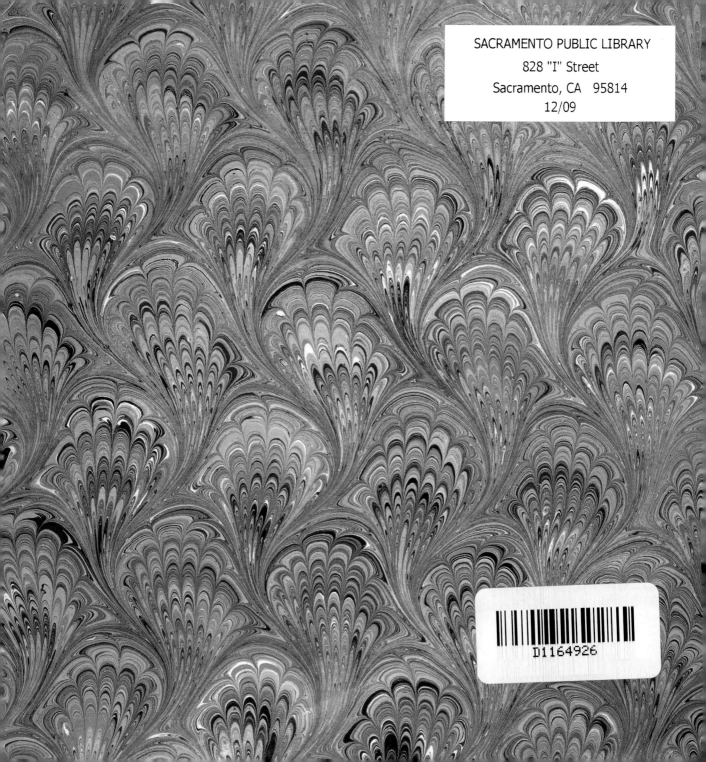

The Luminous Heartbeat

Wendy Victor

The Luminous Heartbeat
Published by Ovation Books
P.O. Box 80107
Austin, TX 78758

For more information about our books, please write to us, call 512.478.2028, or visit our website at www.ovationbooks.net.

Distributed to the trade by National Book Network, Inc.

Publishers Cataloging-in-Publication Data available upon request

Library of Congress Control Number: 2007943711

ISBN-13: 978-0-9790275-7-4
ISBN-10: 0-9790275-7-8

10 9 8 7 6 5 4 3 2 1

Part I—Five Thousand Years of Silence 1

Why women stepped out of the center of power,

and the implication for our time.

Part II—The Genesis Garden 75

Where the myth of Creation is re-visioned through

art and poetry.

Part III—Wings of the Cherubim 125

A simple story of female action in the world.

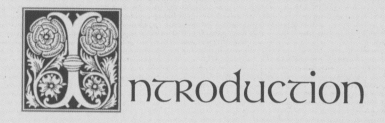

Introduction

Several years ago I was lying on the floor of our fishing camp with Joe, a dear friend who had been Chairman of Philip Morris. We were doing push-ups together. He asked me about our upcoming trip to Africa and why I was going. I replied, "I want to learn from the women."

This was something he simply could not understand. His company, one of the largest in the United States, had for years been giving economic assistance to the peoples of Africa, and he himself was a philanthropist. That we, an advanced nation, had something to learn from these people about culture and community and reverence for life and people—this was not conceivable to him.

I heard him. And yet, there is so much that just does not seem right to me about our Western culture today. Violence against women particularly upsets me.

I started to think that the problem for us in the West, but also for women all over the world, originates in the interpretation of the myth of the Garden of Eden. For, if you believe the approved version, women are responsible for the expulsion from Paradise, Original Sin, and most of the woes that beset not only men but the entire world.

The background that led to the making of this myth, the retelling of the Creation story, and the future in a world that lets go of the negative image of women is the story of *The Luminous Heartbeat.*

I have listed in the bibliographies for each section the books that most influenced my thinking. Over nine years of reading and writing, certain things have changed in the world, but the basic story remains.

It is for us to take action and make a change. I believe that goodness abides, and that we must step forth to reclaim our responsibility for the wellness of our people, and our planet.

She comes walking with visible breath, with visible tracks,
Walking in a sacred manner.
> —From the story of the White Bison Spirit Woman

PART II

FIVE THOUSAND YEARS OF SILENCE

In the beginning there was an end, and connecting the end and the beginning was breath, the living spirit.

The end was not implied in the beginning. There was no separation. All was unity, and the unity was harmony, and the harmony was love.

I tell you a story from all time. It is the wisdom of the elders revealed in the newborn, for in the eyes of the babies we recognize our ancient spirits as we tell these tales to the little ones in our arms.

We come from love and we return to love and we exist all our days in love.

There is no exile from this place and thus no need to return. We are there always.

The breath, the living spirit, washes over us. It blesses us and nourishes us. This is the universal light, the underlying sound, the very vibration of this earth within the cosmos that connects us—

Prologue

What I want to know is—my passion is to discover— what happened in the world, about five thousand years ago, to dethrone Mother Earth and Fertility and the Wise Woman and to allow male-centered religions and male texts and male discourse to dominate our lives. For all the reading I have done over the past almost forty years, until I started to put together this book, I found no answer that satisfied me.

So I decided to go on a quest. To take a journey into the songs and stories of indigenous peoples, and into the history of civilized peoples to see what I could learn from them. I wanted to know about power—about female power within the sacred tradition—because I do believe that the real power of a people, or of a gender, lies in discovering who talks to God.

Because if you are not part of the group that performs the sacraments, and if you are written out of the sacred texts, and if you are not seen as essential to the survival of your people, well, then you have really ceased to exist.[1]

Chapter 1

In the old days there was a duality of dark and light, of evil and good, of destruction and creation that was at the very base of the early society of the goddess and her peoples. Goddesses in Mesopotamian societies had the same attributes as did the gods: they were warlike and blood-thirsty. They demanded sacrifices of limb and life to appease them when they were angry.

The structure of society reflected the pantheon above.[2] Women had real power, and this is completely different from the intercessory power attributed to the Virgin Mary. The power of the Virgin Mary lies in her sexual purity, and the miracle of her virgin conception separates her totally from other women. At the time of the Sacred Marriage, in the old societies women and goddesses had direct power. They waged wars, killed their lovers, husbands, and children. They were vengeful, wrathful, and downright terrifying. The dark power of the female was truly awesome.

These were the days of the ritual of the Sacred Marriage. At the invitation of the goddess, the male was united sexually with the goddess or with her priestess, and the male was sacrificed. His blood was shed on the ground in order to ensure the fertility of the crops and the change of the seasons, so that everything would be right in the world. This was a celebration of fertility, and people believed that the well-being of the land and of the people depended on the sexual intercourse of female and male.[3]

It seems to me that there occurred a huge change in thinking (certainly in the Western world) at this time five thousand years ago in regard to the nature of sexuality. As long as sexuality was seen as good, as pleasing to the goddesses and gods, as part of the sacred offering made in petition of good things to be granted, then there was no sin in the sexual act and no sinfulness in sexuality. The fertilized ground of the womb of the woman was sacred.

What was happening culturally at the time that the female pantheon changed to a single male god, or to exclusively male gods, in several different organized religions? One huge change was that, at this time, writing was developed. Around 2500 B.C. a scribe in a grain storage cylinder in Mesopotamia decided to keep track of his inventory by writing down not pictures but rather symbols based on human sounds.[4] Thus started writing as we know it and, with it, the beginning of recorded history. This early alphabet was used by Hebrews, Phoenicians, Greeks, and was the foundation for all known alphabets.[5]

At the time that this new alphabet was formed, and things were starting to be written down, there was a strong tradition of oral history, of storytelling, that was very different in nature.[6] Instead of the truth or the facts being recorded by one person for posterity, there was an interaction of sound and meaning that occurred each time a story was told, as the teller watched the listener for responses, and stories and history were altered both to be appropriate and to have meaning at that particular time.[7]

We forget these things. We forget that there used to be multiple ways to understand and interact with peoples and animals and that there were things which we could not learn about in books.[8] Even the Book of Genesis records that there was a time when God and animal and human all understood and spoke with each other.

It is difficult to remember, or to research, what written history meant at the time it was recorded. We have little way of knowing what was going on between particular peoples at a particular time—what distractions there might have been; what wonderful sounds or smells may have influenced the scribe; what phase the moon was in; or what may have been going on within their family life on that particular day.

All these things influence the truth of recorded history.

When this new language appeared, there was a strong oral tradition in place, and thus the first large written texts to appear in Greece—namely the *Iliad* and the *Odyssey*—draw heavily on the oral tradition to keep the attention of the audience.

The told story enraptures and captivates.[9]

What does all of this have to do with the change from fertility and sexual celebration of the Sacred Marriage to the male kings and male gods and to the beginning of what some call patriarchy? Can the development of the alphabet, based on human language instead of on pictures, actually be linked to all of this?

I believe it can. The effect of the development of writing and recording history was huge. Some credit it with the beginning of male dominance over women, of the possibility, and then the reality, of supplanting the all-powerful Goddess with a Supreme male God. Others see this as a time when wisdom was lost—Wisdom, in the old tradition. This was a time when a higher faculty and facility of receiving information was supplanted by this new invention of writing, of listening to human sounds and writing these down with a human instrument, held by a human hand.

This was a time when the old symbols were put aside, when depiction of female bodies and fertility objects were discarded in favor of sacred texts written by male scribes and destined for male readers. If the pantheon of deities is a reflection of the power of the people, then the loss of the old symbols truly reflected the change in society as the sacred beings moved from female to male. And so it came to pass that the Word of God was understood to be what created the world and everything in it, and that the oral tradition and cycles of nature and fertility and sexuality—particularly female sexuality—were no longer valued and were cast aside.

Of course, this did not happen overnight. It was a gradual process that took place all over the world; in some countries it happened quickly and others slowly, but it did happen almost everywhere. Only in a few indigenous societies—far from civilization and books and accumulation of knowledge through what is written—is there still a female pantheon and female power in societies and females in the stories of creation and destruction and of the life of the people.

So what am I saying? I am saying that it is possible and, per-haps, likely that some basic change came over the human race at a certain point in history;[10] that the old ways and the old wis-dom were lost; that I, and we, are wanting to recapture it; and that this is the time.

 hapter 2

want to keep coming back to the "why" of why this happened, because that is my passion, and I need to go out and explore, look at what we know, be still and come in touch with what we remember, and then gather that up. Even though I am using the symbols of writing, I am in the storytelling mode. I am having a conversation with you, and I am listening for your response.

There was a shift, I believe, as part of a devaluing of connection and wholeness. As a result of this devaluing, a new symbol was developed, and this appropriated the old symbols.

There were certain physical things happening all over the world five thousand years ago that we simply cannot understand. For instance, we don't understand how the pyramids of Egypt were built or how the temples of the Mayans were erected. It is thought that perhaps people in those days were able to concentrate their mental energy to generate forces that enable them to do things that we are not physically able to do today; that the mental power of peoples acting in unison was greater than that of individuals using tools of modern technology. These ancient peoples most likely had an understanding of force that as yet we do not grasp or remember.[11]

I believe that it is the invention of the alphabet that served to separate us from the wisdom of this natural world, that allied us with the Word of a male God, and that created this huge separation between humans and the rest of what is out there.

Writing did not cause this to happen; writing was merely the new symbol that came into being to replace the old symbols: the oral tales, the interactive mode of learning and knowing, and the fertility cult figures.

God, and then humans, started to use these "words" to name things, to give them their distinctness. And this separation caused divisions and hierarchies: of God from Satan; of God from what He created; of God from Adam, and then Adam from Eve; of light and dark; and good from evil. It caused division of the human body itself, or rather, the cultural values in many societies created a division, with the head being associated with God and intelligence and man, and the lower half being associated with woman and Satan and sexuality.[12]

The more we uncover about ancient civilizations all over the world, the more likely does this theory about the importance of language and the writing and recording of history seem to

me. The sensuous world was regarded as the dwelling place of
the gods. It was here, in light and
mystery and darkness, that they
moved, seized their loves, and
drank the blood of their victims.
In the light of day, in the books
written by monks in the monas-

teries, the wildness and willfulness of the gods and goddesses
was relegated to the flatness of the page. A fuller use of faculties,
a closeness with nature—a pagan connection, if you will—was
lost about five thousand years ago.

What is the effect of these pictorially derived systems? Of
writing? Well, they demand a shift away from voice and gesture,
and from understanding what the land and the animals are telling us. We focused on what we were writing down, told ourselves

what we needed to know in history, and declared that what we were writing was the ultimate truth.

The "truth" of the male texts—the male-written sacred texts that order the world in their own way—has to do with hierarchies, with God over man and man over woman and human over animals. This is the modern way of thinking, a way of separation and exclusion and destruction, of power over others being valued instead of unity and connection and healing. It all did go together, in the old days, but there was a balance and a cycle to the seasons of nature, to spilling of blood and semen and fertility and childbirth, to death and sacrifice and the ensuing renewal of the land. And no one thing ever had ascendancy over another for ever and ever, nor does it now.

hapter 3

What happened to the power of the woman, and the Goddess, when the male took over the ability to both create and procreate? In a sense, to replicate himself? According to history, at this time the male god made a covenant with the males of His chosen people, and this ritual of the covenant was for males only.[13] It had to do with circumcision of male children, and it said that the chosen people of this God would be known by the physical appearance of the male procreative member.

I find it interesting that women are totally absent from this covenant between God and His people.[14] It just reconfirms for me that the struggle in the Hebrew text is about the ascendancy of the male over the female, about Yahweh edging out Sophia, Adam laying the blame on Eve, and about the change in the pantheon above and society below.

The big thing—the most important symbol that men appropriated—was the ability of male to create male.[15] No females needed. In both versions of the creation story in Genesis, God creates first man and woman, and then man alone, *without the help of a female.*[16] The Word of God creates instead of the female egg fertilized by the male sperm. Written history supplants the oral traditions and the old ways of knowing the underlying connections within the universe.

Synonymous with this male begetting male and disconnection with the natural processes observed in nature was that, in Genesis, the animals no longer speak. In the Garden, the serpent spoke to the woman, and she understood him. And the man understood the woman, and God spoke directly to His people, and they all understood each other. So, one common language.

The power that shamans and goddesses used—the greater perception of sounds and sights they called upon in their magic and healing—had now been obliterated from the proper order of creation and the world under one male God.

So it came to pass that the divine marriage, the sexual intercourse between female and male, gave way to a new type of conjugal relation—the marriage between God and His people.[17] In this union, the life of the people comes not from an agrarian rite of sacred marriage but from the intervention of Yahweh in the history of his people and the world. And the intervention is for the sheer purpose of making history, not to make fertile the earth and to perpetuate the cycles of nature and the closeness of all animate and inanimate things.

I want to go to the Bible, to part of it that I really love, a part that resonates in every part of me—to the Song of Songs.

That the Song of Songs is included in the canon of the Bible is, in itself, quite extraordinary. There was quite a struggle over its inclusion in the male text, but here it is, with the old tradition of the Goddess and fertility, with both desire for and joy in sexual union.[18] Even though, throughout time, there have been varied interpretations of the meaning of the Song of Songs, recent scholarship is moving away from the allegorical interpretation, which sanitizes the lust. I, for one, find meaning in linking this portion of the Hebrew Bible back to the older religions of the goddess.[19]

I understand that there was a struggle to calm the revelries of the pagans: their love feasts, which included drunkenness, gluttony, incest and cannibalism, among others.[20] It just seems that the control may have gone too far and, in curbing the excesses, males and their scribes took away the power of fertility and the natural connection to the earth.

But I am getting ahead of myself.

"Three times a day a miracle took place with the wings of the Cherubim.

When the holiness of the King revealed itself over them, the Cherubim, of themselves, stretched out their wings and covered their bodies with them. A cloud descended and when it settled over the Lid, the wings of the Cherubim intertwined and they beat them and sang a song."[21]

Oh, I long for the song. The Song of Songs. The dance of the earth; the dance of the Lord Shiva that turns the earth into creation. I long for the ancient mysteries, the old knowledge. I long for the primal blessedness, for the union with the divine, and for the acknowledgment of the divine in all of us, and in everything about us.

Chapter 4

Do we need to rewrite, or retell, or re-vision the story of Genesis and all that follows in the Hebrew and the Christian Bible? Maybe. Yes. In a way, this is the ultimate act, in modern society, for a woman to take back the power. She must reinterpret the sacred texts. By doing so, she is rewriting history, back to the time when writing was first invented and used by men to create their own sacred symbols to tell their story—to *make* their story.

I need the sacred—and the cultic—in my life. I like the linkage of the Song of Songs with *One Thousand and One Nights.* The storytelling is what moves me. I get caught up with the people; I want to know how it all turns out.

In the third century fragment of the Gospel of Mary, there exists a story—or part of a story—that tells how Mary Magdalene strengthens the courage of the disciples to preach the gospel. It appears that, in the written version, at the request of Peter she also tells them of some private teaching she received from Jesus.[22] (Unfortunately several pages of her speech have been lost.)

No kidding. Just imagine what would happen to a male-dominated religion that puts women in a subservient role, removes them from performing the sacred traditions, and commands them to silence in God's presence, if somewhere in the canon of the Bible it recorded Jesus' words giving the sexually active woman authority to pass on the word of God.

I find it absolutely terrifying that the crucial pages are missing from the Book of Mary. This keeps happening. When I was working at the Convent of the Sacred Heart in Greenwich, Connecticut, I had a video showing paintings in the catacombs under St. Peter's in Rome. These paintings depicted women acting as priests—giving the sacrament—in the first years of Christianity.

The video disappeared.

Where did we let go of our desire for our beloved, as we know it in the Song of Songs?[23]

I need to remember about the sacredness of place.

In Australia, there are all these "song lines" crisscrossing the land, and the Aboriginal women guard their knowledge of the sacred songs. They tap the magic and the power from these ancient sources in the land itself, and they guard their knowledge from the men.[24]

Place matters. Our surroundings speak to us. This is the ancient wisdom that we know: it does matter what happens in our families and homes, in our communities and nations.

Perhaps that is why I had to move from Connecticut to Florida to write what I needed to write. For many years I have known that I worked best barefoot; that I needed to touch the carpet or the wood or the earth under my feet in order to think, to feel, to know deeply. My husband put pipes for hot water under the wooden floorboards in the writing cottage he built for me in Connecticut, so that in the winter I could work without my shoes on.

Language and story are tied to the land. That is the great wisdom of all the shamans. To access wisdom, you need to be able to listen to the earth itself, and then to speak and act on the very margins of what can be known and dreamed and imagined. It is the cosmic dance pulsing in the vibrations of the earth.

And the language that comes out of this process is inseparable from song and story. The songs and stories, in their turn, are inseparable from the land.

What the move from oral tales to written history did, there-fore, is make this process of interaction between human and plant and animal rigid; it separated the human out of the natu-ral world. And that is the very problem we are struggling with in so many places today.

Chapter 5

There is a wisdom for me in the land in Ethiopia. I do believe that the Ark of the Covenant is there in the Church of Mary in Axum. It is a holy land of women.

It is here that the embrace of the Cherubim on the Lid of the Ark of the Covenant shows the sacredness and importance of the sexual embrace of male and female. This sexual embrace of female and male is what literally hovered over—physically hovered over—the first written Word of Yahweh.

Think about that.

The Wings of the Cherubim beat a song as they hovered over the Ark of the Covenant.

What is this nonsense we have been told to believe, that women are not crucial to creation, holiness, and to the life of the people?

The Ark of the Covenant, with the female Cherubim sitting on its roof, was carried into battle—over and over and over—to give victory against the enemy.

The Shekinah is so powerful that her *kiss* brings death.

The pain, the sadness, of the exile of Adam and Eve from the Garden.[25]

This comes from the shift away from the land and into the realm of the Word and the Finger of God writing history. It seems to me that the loss is precisely the loss of feminine relatedness and connection, that underlying unity of all things that we knew when there was One instead of Zero, or nothingness.[26]

This is the same as Hildegard of Bingen's vision of the Church as Mother, a life-giving aspect which she likens to "greenness."[27]

What I see today is many women returning to the earth. I am—by moving to a place of endless summer, of forever all-year birds and flowers and green grass. It gives me joy and opens me up, and I can work and write and make connections with people I love.

One of my daughters is an environmental lawyer; the other has worked as a writer for Audubon and for *National Geographic* and is setting out now to write and travel in Southeast Asia for three months.

There is a revaluing of how we can, and must, care for our lands.

The loss of Paradise may be understood as a loss of this unity with nature. The exile I understand as God's exile from his female companion, from Astarte or Sophia or the Shekinah.

The sexual union implied in the Song of Songs where woman desires man and this is good and joyful is reversed in the Book of Genesis, where woman's sexuality is sinful, as it leads man astray and results in a loss of grace.

I don't think so.

There was an original community of integrated knowledge, one wherein there was a common language.[28] One wherein the serpent—the old wisdom—was trying to teach us something, and wanted us to eat from the Tree of Knowledge. I believe that the male God created by male writers grew jealous, or fearful—or that males who recorded this history grew jealous, or fearful, and understood this gift of the serpent as something evil.

Denial of the flesh, it seems to me, is really the pivotal point where the Goddess was abandoned, where unity with nature was turned away from, and where we reduced the wide input of our senses and our rhythms, and our ancient knowledge, and let it be for men to use the abstract symbols of written language to make their version of the truth.

The joining up of the sacred—in human and animal life, in story and in myth and in history—is where we need to go to remember our strength.

What I find is that women want to know. They want to find meaning for all this. They want to talk.[29]

They need images—role models, sacred beings—that reveal and strengthen the sacred within us.

I need to look at, and know, women of deep feminine beauty and grace. I actively seek them out and try to put them in my life.

Some men, especially some men with strongly developed feminine natures and sensibilities, recognize and nurture this part of me.

So why were the ancient mother-goddesses rejected in favor of male gods? I must answer this. Can it just be the fear of our dark side? Fear of our terrible power? Was woman's lust for semen truly insatiable?

Relationship is what lets us understand the underlying unity of all things. Relationship with male; relationship with female; relationship with the earth; and with the cosmos. The Egyptian goddess Nut every day gives birth to the sun, and every evening she destroys what she has created.[30] This is the female principle of creation and destruction, that awesome power we have turned away from.

I believe we want to return home—home to the sacred; home to the Garden; home to a world of oneness and unity and grace.

The longing for God—for union with the divine—seems to be the ultimate wish. Is death the necessary condition for union with the divine? Does this confirm the Sacred Marriage?

How do I reconnect?

Language matters. Words matter. I intentionally say "women and men," half the time, and then "men and women," the other half. I do not say "mankind," and do not refer to the act of creation as "seminal." I listen a lot and read a lot and try to speak with intention. In my own way, like Emily Dickinson, I create my own discourse.[31] For me, having a voice is a direct result of having a language.[32]

I choose to connect my mind and my body. I choose to feel, to connect the sensuous and the spiritual, to acknowledge that I am a sacred being, and then I choose to honor that of which I am a part.

The longer I make a disconnection, the greater is the gap between the person I am creating—my persona—and the person I am at my core. The gap may get so big that I cannot go back. I forget where home is, or even that I have a home.

Another way to return to who we are is to tell our stories.[33] To tell the stories of women who are strong, of women who have power, without telling the story in anger. I love and seek out women who move in their lives with that deep femininity that speaks of honoring the sacred, of valuing people and relationships as primary.

Ceremony and ritual express connection to the natural world. And that world, in turn, is understood through story, dream, and prophecy.

There is a myth, an old myth, in Australia about how women lost their sacred power.

According to the story told by the Djanggawul peoples, among the ancient ancestors it was women who first had the sacred implements and the sacred songs. The power of the women lay in these sacred songs, and the women carried the emblems of their power in their uteri.

One day the Sisters went swimming and laid their "dilly bags," as they referred to their uteri, on the river bank. The men had been lying in wait, watching for this moment, and seized their bags and made off with them. And, according to the myth, when the theft was discovered, the younger (sister) said to the elder, "What are we going to do? All our dilly bags are gone, all the emblems, all our power for sacred ritual!" But the other replied, "I think we can leave that. Men can do it now; they can look after it. We can spend our time collecting bush foods for them, for it is not right that they should get that food as they have been doing. We know everything. We have really lost nothing, for we remember it all, and we can let them have that small part."[34]

I'm not saying that we are special because we can carry and give birth to children; it's so much more than that. What I am saying is that we have forgotten the old stories and, in the forgetting, have lost the sense of our own innate sacredness.

And, in forgetting the old stories, we have forgotten our wisdom and our deep femininity and our ability to keep the earth and its peoples in wellness.

Chapter 6

If we are to tell our stories and pass on our wisdom, we need to recapture our authentic voices. I remember being on a plane, going from New York to San Francisco. I was in the small first-class section; there was a young baby, maybe three or four months old, howling its head off. The voice was powerful, deep, resonant. I was astonished to find out that it belonged to a girl; it taught me a lesson. We are not born quiet. We are taught to become that way.

The process of attuning to these rhythms of living is in the storytelling. The process of attuning the rhythm of one's life always involves storytelling.[35]

The very symbols of our religions are closing off the songs of the universe.

The Christian belief in hierarchy and separation stands in direct contrast to the beliefs in goddesses, which imply an underlying realization of the unity of all things. Goddesses, by their very nature, embody the principle of unity.

When a hierarchy of body and spirit was created, there was made a separation of sensual and spiritual, and the rite of the Sacred Marriage was broken.

Most polytheistic cultures are aware of the unity of all life. That is why the different aspects of life are honored through naming of various divinities. If there is a rhythm to life—of light and dark, birth and death, female and male—then that pulse between opposites is the very essence of life, and, it seems to me, that this is what the Christians have forgotten.

Eroticism simply had to be taken out of sexuality and fertility so that the concept of Original Sin, repentance, and atonement could take hold. The paradigm of the culture had to shift from life-enhancing to death-promoting.

The development of hierarchy helped to make this shift, with the upper body and reason being associated with male, and the lower half with sensuality and female.

One thing I think about in connection with all this is how it relates to overpopulation, disease, poverty, and the growing depletion of natural, life-sustaining resources. It seems to me that there was some large cycle in place that had to do with the de-emphasizing of sexuality and fertility—and that now, maybe, with the slow revaluing of the sacredness in life, the cycle is turning.

With this remembering of the sacred, there comes the recognition that the deep feminine values of relatedness must and do apply to the harmony of all living things and to this planet and beyond.

I think that Western civilization developed in this great cycle, and that the devaluing of women in relation to the sacred was the created symbol to bring this about.

Why do we choose to leave ourselves out of the story, out of history? Why did we give our voice, our power, our sacred self away?[36]

I believe it is because we were not willing to accept our dark side, our side that destroys and kills, that takes life away. For five thousand years we have been denying this part of ourselves, and in the process we have become so very out of balance.

Remember that the basis for the ritual of the Sacred Marriage was the belief that when the Goddess was happy and satisfied, she blessed the land and the people. More often than not, the sacred union was followed by the death of the young god. This combination of semen and blood, of life-creating and death-producing, was the essential nature of the duality of the Goddess. This same duality was observable in nature with the following of light and dark, the seasons, and the decay and regrowth of all living things.

The essential equality of women could not be banished from thought and feeling as long as the goddesses lived and were believed to rule human life.[37]

I learn from the East, from the Chinese, from their unity of yin and yang, about how opposites complement each other. They find a balance that is dynamic.

The power of the Virgin Mary lies in being the Dark Madonna. The power of Chartres Cathedral lies in its incorporation of the Dark Madonna and the Druids that are at the very base of its foundation.

That's what woman does—the deep feminine—she blesses and touches and makes connection. She has the power to destroy, but she chooses not to. That's the courtesy that woman wants—the power to choose for herself.

When she is attacked, now, she retreats in silence. It's been going on for so long.

Oh, I know, there are feminists and activists and women's movements and women's anger. I've studied that; I've lived that. What I mean is something quite different, this search for the strong feminine within us. It's quiet and deep and strong. We see it in the women of many indigenous cultures, the ones who make kings and lead tribal councils. Those women who call themselves the hope and the future of the nations.[38] Those are the ones who need to come out of their silence, to drop the mantle of mystery and darkness and safety and come out into the light. The *spirit* of these women is so strong.

The Sioux men put rabbit skins on their arms and legs so they can take on the qualities of the rabbit—soft, quiet, humble, not self-asserting—when they go to the center of the world.[39] And are these not the qualities that women have been asked to take on? But not so they can attain entrance to the spirit world, rather so they can be marginalized by their peoples.

Many cultures, and many civilizations, have tried to make women pure and humble. Many men—and many women—see women as being that way. The vessel of a woman's body, in particular the womb of a woman—has been likened to a sacred vessel, or to the Holy Grail. I think this is so. The power and the mystery flow into us and grow in darkness.

I think, over these five thousand years, that we have been letting this happen, unwilling to bring forth that which we bear. Our gift, our wisdom—we have been holding this back.

After I turned fifty, I started to know that I know. It's just a feeling, but I'm absolutely sure of it when it comes. And it comes more and more often. I just see what is the next right thing to do, or to say.

I recently read *The Rape of Nanking* by Iris Chang. Wonderful book. I was struck by what she says about the victims themselves having remained silent, and how this caused this horrific event not to "penetrate" (her word) world consciousness.

Right. This is how things are erased from memory. The women remain silent. Nothing has happened.

She says that there is "not a word" about this event in Winston Churchill's *Memoirs of the Second World War.*[40]

Interesting, what this silence can do.

I've spent fifty years of my life being silent about some things that have happened to me during my life. I knew that certain things were wrong, yet I did not speak out.

I don't believe in trying to undo the past or in acting out in anger or in trying to assign blame at this point. I've moved beyond that. It's just that I can see now what the silence does.

For me, now, it all comes back to where we are in the sacred tradition of each of our cultures. One thing seems pretty obvious: when all positions of prestige within a religion are allocated to males, and confined to males, then there are far-reaching implications both socially and spiritually for women.[41] If we are letting ourselves be second-class citizens in religious biases, including being seen as the person who caused the Fall and led man into sin; if we give up our sacred role as Mother and Goddess and Bringer of both Life and Death; if we choose to remain silent and renounce who and what we are—well, then, do you see what happens to the people and to the planet?

In the long history of the human race, male dominance of religious roles is a pretty recent development. It's about five thousand years old. Before that, women were the divine figures, and they did interpret the divine message for humans.

Once written language—the new symbols—appeared, then things did absolutely change. Men wrote the religious literature. Men guarded not only the sacred texts, but also the power to interpret them, as well as the right to handle the sacred objects.

What women could do to gain status within this new construct was to give up their sexuality.[42] By remaining virgins, by abandoning the role of wife and mother, these women could exempt themselves from being treated as women.

By being meek, submissive, quiet, they were granted status.[43]

Some price.

So many societies ask men to protect women to control their sexuality. To take the male name when they marry; to keep them quiet; to make laws that keep them from owning property in their own name.

I *chose*, at the age of forty-six, to take up my husband's name. With great pleasure. For we were forming an active unit, and I wanted to be part of it. I was—and am—happy to share this "we" that we have made.

And there was so much in my old life that I wanted to leave behind. This was a new beginning, and I'm grateful to my husband for offering to share his life with me. Today I also value who I am and know that I am bringing him an equal blessing.

The thing is, I had a choice. That's the main thing.

Chapter 7

So, to go back to the goddesses and their sexuality, and to the fertility of peoples and of the earth. It seems that the early women were deemed good because of their sexuality and fertility, and then, when formal, male-centered religions developed, women were seen as *bad* because of their sexuality and fertility.[44]

In the *Kebra Nagast*, it seems that at the moment of sexual intercourse and consummation between Solomon and the Queen of Sheba, that Solomon saw the presence of God depart from him and Israel and pass on to the new Israel that would be established in Africa.[45].

Is it a wonder that the Ark of the Covenant is supposed to have left the Temple of Solomon and have been taken to Ethiopia to the Temple of Mary of Zion? Feminine wisdom—the ancient Sophia—was transferred to the proper place.

The Ark is represented in every church in Ethiopia by a *tabot*, a stone tablet placed inside a wooden chest.[46]

The dedication of the Church of Mary in Axum to Zion may suggest that Axum came to be regarded as the new Jerusalem.

Women seem to have a particular facility with words, with spoken language. I find that Emily Dickinson's extraordinarily new usage of *written* language is based on her different breathing patterns. Most women tend to speak in shorter sentences than men; they pause more often, let the spaces carry as much weight and meaning as the audible part. I think this comes from our long history as storytellers—of using silences for emphasis, and for mystery and drama. Dickinson's pauses—her hyphens—break absolutely the rhythm of male language.

In my years of work on Emily Dickinson, I came to find that I could grasp her meaning in both her letters and poems if I read them aloud. My ear could hear the movement between the known and the unknown worlds; the meaning was permeable if I used the mode of the storyteller and the listener.

I became familiar with the meaning she attached to words, and how her lexicon changed over time. Texture, depth, subtle changes were perceptible to my ear, rather than just to my mind. What I find now is that this expansion of sensory awareness, this ability of the shamans to listen to plants and animals and things of another world, are present in the language of Emily Dickinson.

Of course we remember that the earliest shamans seem to have been exclusively women.[47]

So, as organized religion became stronger, women's voices became weaker, and women's visions—this ancient shamanic ability—were only considered seriously by the Christians when these women were celibate, and preferably virgins.[48]

Interesting.

How did we let things get so turned around that St. Augustine was allowed to proclaim that a wife's duty is to serve her husband even if he beats her?[49]

The Gnostic Gospels tell us that Sophia, the old Wisdom, gave Adam breath, a soul, and her daughter Eve to be his instructor.[50]

In *The Golden Legend*, a book of the Middle Ages, we find that women martyrs, usually virgins, were threatened with different tortures than the men. They were inevitably stripped nude, threatened with rape—when they were not actually raped—and frequently had their breasts torn off.[51]

That's a lot of fear of the power of female sexuality, whether the women are female martyrs, clinging to their celibacy and virginity in order to have a voice under Roman laws, or are the pagan temptresses who seduce men and lead them into sin.

pilogue

I return to the sacred, from whence I came.

In the ancient texts of the Upanishads, women's desire is not for men, or for blood or for power. It is for spiritual knowledge.[52]

I believe that nothing has changed. I think we have just forgotten and have become terribly sidetracked. My very being thirsts for spiritual knowledge. I love some of the material things, the luxuries for the body and for the senses—but I choose to dwell with beauty as part of my connection to the life of the spirit.

I agree with Alice Walker, in *The Color Purple,* that our great sin—perhaps our only sin—is not to live in joy in the beauty of this world.

I want us to reclaim our symbols. To define our language. To bring back our storytelling and our ancient wisdom. It's as simple, and as monumental, as that.

I want to tell my story and to tell it well. For that gives you courage and throws you back on your own wisdom and lets you know that there are others—many, many others—traveling on this path, and that this telling of our story is the most important thing we can ever do.

We carry the Wisdom of the wise women who have gone before us. We know that we know. We carry those songs, and those stories, in the very heart of our being.[53]

It is time. The powerful feminine is called home.

ACKNOWLEDGMENT

This work would simply not have been possible without my husband Mike. At every step of the way he has encouraged me: to go to graduate school and pursue my path in women's history; to dare to stand against both women and men when needed; to allow me the space to breathe and grow and explore; and ultimately, to journey into spiritual territory.

And, for my friends and family who help me and love me and believe in me, this book is for you—Rebecca and Dora and Jenny and Deirdre. For Leslie, who teaches me about the world, and for Laura, who gives me my voice. For Elizabeth, Debbie, Winifred. For Denis and Spencer. And for so many others. You strengthen me in ways that bless me. Thank you.

Note on the photographs:

Taken on the Amazon River in Peru, 1999, by the author

Bibliography

FIVE THOUSAND YEARS OF SILENCE

Abram, David. *The Spell of the Sensuous: Perception and Language in a More-Than-Human World.* New York: Vintage Books, 1996.

Allen, Paula Gunn. *The Sacred Hoop: Recovering the Feminine in American Indian Traditions.* Beacon Press, 1986.

Baker, Denise Nowakowski. *Julian of Norwich's Showings: From Vision to Book*. Princeton: Princeton University Press, 1994.

Bonheim, Jalaja, ed. *Goddess: A Celebration in Art and Literature*. New York: Stewart, Tabori and Chang, 1997.

Brown, Joseph Epes, recorder and ed. *The Sacred Pipe: Black Elk's Account of the Seven Rites of the Ogala Sioux*. Norman: University of Oklahoma Press, 1953.

Buss, Fran Leeper, ed. *Forged Under the Sun: The Life of Maria Elena Lucas*, Ann Arbor: The University of Michigan Press, 1993.

Chang, Iris. *The Rape of Nanking: The Forgotten Holocaust of World War II*. New York: Basic Books, 1997.

Dalrymple, William. *From the Holy Mountain: A Journey Among the Christians of the Middle East*. New York: Henry Holt and Company, 1997.

Davidson, Robyn. *From Alice to Ocean: Alone Across the Outback.* New York: Addison-Wesley Publishing Company, 1992.

Deloria, Ella Cara. *Waterlily.* Lincoln: University of Nebraska Press, 1988.

Deloria, Vine Jr. and Lytle, Clifford. *The Nations Within: The Past and Future of American Indian Sovereignty.* New York: Pantheon Books, 1984.

Eisler, Riane. *The Chalice and the Blade: Our History, Our Future.* San Francisco: Harper San Francisco, 1987.

Estes, Clarissa Pinkola, Ph.D. *Women Who Run with the Wolves: Myths and Stories of the Wild Woman Archetype.* New York: Ballantine Books, 1992.

Gilchrist, Roberta. *Gender and Material Culture: The archaeology of religious women.* New York: Routledge, 1994.

Gilligan, Carol. *In a Different Voice: Psychological Theory and Women's Development.* Cambridge: Harvard University

Press, 1982.

Gutierrez, Ramon A. *When Jesus Came, the Corn Mothers Went Away: Marriage, Sexuality, and Power in New Mexico,1500-1846.* Stanford, California: Stanford University Press, 1991.

Hancock, Graham. *The Sign and the Seal: The Quest for the Lost Ark of the Covenant.* New York: Simon & Schuster, Inc., 1992.

Hawass, Zahi. *Silent Images: Women in Pharaonic Egypt.* Cairo: Ministry of Culture, Cultural Development Fund, 1995.

Helman, Marilyn. *African Zion: The Sacred Art of Ethiopia.* New Haven: Yale University Press, 1993.

Hunt, Lynn. *The Family Romance of the French Revolution.* Berkeley: University of California Press, 1992.

Huxley, Elspeth. *The Flame Trees of Thika.* London: Penguin Books, 1959.

Johnson, Robert A. *Femininity Lost and Regained.* New York: Harper & Row, Publishers, 1990.

Kapchan, Deborah A. *Gender on the Market: Moroccan Women and the Revoicing of Tradition.* Philadelphia: University of Pennsylvania Press, 1996.

Katz, Jane, ed. *Messengers of the Wind: Native American Women Tell Their Life Stories.* New York: Ballantine Books, 1995.

Lawlor, Robert. *Sacred Geometry: Philosophy and Practice.* London: Thames and Hudson, Ltd., 1982.

Lerner, Gerda. *The Creation of Patriarchy.* New York: Oxford University Press, 1986.

——*The Creation of Feminist Consciousness from the Middle Ages to Eighteen-seventy.* New York: Oxford University Press, 1993.

——*Why History Matters: Life and Thought.* New York: Oxford University Press, 1997.

McLynn, Frank. *Carl Gustav Jung*. New York: St. Martin's Press, 1997.

McNamara, Jo Ann Kay. *Sisters in Arms: Catholic Nuns Through Two Millennia*. Cambridge, Massachusetts: Harvard University Press, 1996.

Noonan, Peggy. *Life, Liberty and the Pursuit of Happiness*. New York: Random House, 1994.

Pipher, Mary. *Reviving Ophelia: Saving the Selves of Adolescent Girls*. New York: Ballantine Books, 1994.

Pope, Marvin. *Song of Songs: A New Translation with Introduction and Commentary*. Garden City, New York: Doubleday and Company, Inc., 1977.

Report of the Secretary-General. *From Nairobi to Beijing: Second Review and Appraisal of the Implementation of the Nairobi Forward-Looking Strategies for the Advancement of Women*. New York: United Nations, 1995.

Rhys, Jean. *Good Morning, Midnight.* New York: W.W. Norton & Company, 1986 (first published in 1938).

——*Voyage in the Dark.* New York: W.W. Norton & Company, 1982.

Sabbagh, Suha, ed. *Arab Women: Between Defiance and Restraint.* New York: Interlink Publishing Group, Inc., 1996.

Scholem, Gershom. *On the Kabbalah and Its Symbolism.* New York: Schocken Books, 1996.

Shanks, Hershel. *The Mystery and Meaning of the Dead Sea Scrolls.* New York: Random House Inc., 1998.

Stark, Rodney. *The Rise of Christianity: How the Obscure, Marginal Jesus Movement Became the Dominant Religious Force in the Western World in a Few Centuries.* San Francisco: Harper San Francisco, 1997.

Talhami, Ghada Hashem. *The Mobilization of Muslim Women in Egypt.* Gainesville: University Press of Florida, 1996.

The New Jerusalem Bible. Pocket ed. New York: Doubleday, 1993.

United Nations Office at Vienna. *Women in Politics and Decision-Making in the Late Twentieth Century.* New York: United Nations Publications, 1994.

Victor, Wendy F. "Passion and Power: Emily Dickinson's Garden of Verse." New York: State University of New York, Purchase, 1993.

Wall, Steve. *Wisdom's Daughters: Conversations with Women Elders of North America.* New York: Harper Collins, 1993.

Ware, Susan, ed. "New Viewpoints in Women's History: Working Papers from the Schlesinger Library 50th Anniversary Conference, March 4–5, 1994." Cambridge, Massachusetts, 1994.

West, Cornel. Introduction to *Africa: The Art of the Continent, 100 Works of Power and Beauty.* New York: Guggenheim

Museum, in association with Harry N. Abrams, 1995. Published in conjunction with the exhibition "Africa: The Art of the Continent" shown at the Solomon R. Guggenheim Museum.

Wilson, Colin. *From Atlantis to the Sphinx*. New York: Fromm International Publishing Corporation, 1996.

Woolf, Virginia. *Three Guineas*. New York: Harcourt Brace and Company, 1966. First published in 1938.

Young, Serenity, ed. *An Anthology of Sacred Texts by and about Women*. New York: Crossroad, 1995.

Zinsser, Judith P. *History and Feminism: A Glass Half Full*. New York: Twayne Publishers, 1993.

PART II

THE GENESIS GARDEN

Prologue

The world is all these shades of gray, suffused with light, hidden shapes, and meanings. And in the breath that stretches over the land and its people, I feel the presence of God. I do believe that within each one of us is the divine light, the womb of the world—the Holy Grail, as it were—and this is at once the hope and the redemption of the world.

Bringing the full senses back into the Church is where my heart is today.

In *Five Thousand Years of Silence*, I struggled with remembering and regaining our female voice. I sought to answer why we had lost our power five thousand years ago and found that we had indeed chosen to give it away because we were lonely in our songdream.

And I found that God, too, is in this state of loneliness, having lost his Wise Woman, his Astarte, his Shekinah.

So now this quest goes on. It is about giving woman back her action, having found both her voice and her history. It is about finding ways to reinterpret and rewrite the sacred texts so that we can restore the sense of balance and original unity and wholeness that is so very vital to the planet.

This is our work.

Over the last two years I've done a lot of reading about the Black Virgin, the Holy Grail, the brothers of Jesus, the Gnostic Gospels, and Rosslyn Chapel. I find there are stories about them; I like best the ones that are hidden. I like the mixtures of fact and fiction, books like *The Red Tent* by Ann Diamant and *The Da Vinci Code,* for they cross boundaries and, for me, find a freedom of voice that is often lacking in pure scholarly manuscripts.

And I have come to believe that Mary Magdalene and all she stands for—higher knowledge, the divine priestess, the most beloved of the Disciples—has been hidden behind the personage of the Virgin Mary. And while for a time she has allowed her true nature to be obscured, she is now ready to come forth in her full power. I believe that all the Ave Marias, the name heard most often over this entire land, has all along been a call to her to reveal her true self.

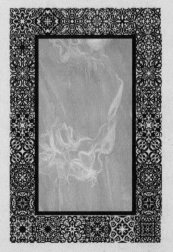

Chapter One

I have had a dream that moves this book forward. It's about the Church, the Divine Embrace, and the eros and energy attraction between a male priest and myself.

Thirty-three years ago I acted on this impulse. Widowed but a week, I joined with the senior pastor of my church. Whether it was sex or love, I know not. What it did was put me on a path to becoming alive again instead of half-dead. To him—both a man of the cloth and a Jungian analyst—I became his anima, the personification of his inner femininity, and he eventually sought to destroy me.[54]

Before that happened, I bought a house for us in Pebble Beach, California, overlooking the restless sea. I gave him money; he used it to buy himself a car and gave the old one to his wife.

His wife wanted a divorce. They had been down this path many times before; they agreed. I sold my house in Connecticut, arranged for schools in California for my children, sold off most of the things in the house, and had a mover pack us up.

The day before we left, the minister changed his mind.

I gave him his ring back, but it didn't end there. I ended up, after it went back and forth between us for another year, having a nervous breakdown, and he was defrocked by the Church.

So, today, when I had the same kind of dream about our pastor, it got my attention. I deeply respect and care for his wife. I am a sober person today. I adore my husband and have no desire for disruption.

And I have learned over the years from my spiritual mother, Winifred, that dreams come to teach us things, to point the way, to show us in a different dimension what we need to know. They are not meant to be taken literally.

Occasionally, very rarely, they are totally precious. These are the mythic dreams. I have these mythic dreams, and I believe this one about the Church and the male priest is one of them.

Other mythic dreams that I remember:

Jesus in the cradle in Scotland, caring for himself and the two Virgin mothers. The other Mary is black and has a daughter.

A dream of the music—the sound of the earth—coming from underground.

Carl Jung talks about thinking in primordial images, in symbols that are older than historical man.

I've been working on research for *The Genesis Garden*, thinking of power and loss and of the role of the female in creation and destruction. I have thought of our sexuality, how we bring forth life, and of our deep and abiding relationship with the male.

The Blanchefleur roses are planted in the garden. The ancient French symbols of red and white, blood and purity.[55]

This time, I do not need to take the dream literally. I know—and feel—the life-giving attraction between the spirit and the body, the female and the male, and the male and the female. I will not connect the mind and the man, and the body and the female. We both have both. And I do not believe that the pull is toward androgyny or toward union with the same sex. No, rather it is the polar pull that gives both life and death, the endless cycle of rebirth, the simultaneous longing for both the Divine Embrace and the rejection of desire.

I feel this in my life in the simplest ways. I like to wear pants—but with pearls and perfume. I feel very feminine with my hair cropped short. I feel connected to the earth being mostly barefoot, but then I like to go out in pretty, high, very feminine sling-back heels.

Of course, I am a Gemini, but it is much more than this. Today I had a letter to the editor published in the *Daily News*. I take the power to myself. I take responsibility for my own opinions today, and am not afraid to voice them. I am finding my voice.

So I dreamt of the minister, and he said something about two women whose faces were made up and their hair colored, and how the artifice was not appealing. How strange our dreams are. Just five days ago when I was having my hair cut, Justin asked if I would ever think of coloring my hair. I said no; I had tried that before for twenty-five years.

And, finally, now I am comfortable with who I am. Losing twenty-five pounds over this past winter and spring makes me feel really good about my body, and I am happy to be sixty. It's

an awesome age. I feel strong, sexy, both loving and caring, and truly able to act in the world.

Of course, I still get decked, as I did just two days ago when the garden appeared to be ruined. I care passionately about it—as does Mike—and we were deeply upset. But things were made right—people took responsibility and replanted—and I know I will be able to write there shortly.

It's all about alchemy. It's about how things interact with each other—the life-energy, the fusion with the divine.

I've noticed the past four or five years that after sex the interaction of male and female energy inside of me activates me for hours afterward. I cannot go to sleep; my mind races, my body is charged, my creative juices are flowing.

No longer able to produce a new life from within myself, this process of uniting opposites seeks an outlet and, after menopause, this seems to have turned from the physical to the mental and spiritual.

No wonder wise-women in many cultures only become so after their midlife change.[56]

The male, on the other hand, is spent after his single life force leaves his body. He must rest and regenerate new energy from within.

For many years—twenty-five—I have been obsessed with color. I have sought to find one static answer, one absolute truth, for which colors I looked best in. This has taken different paths, but all have been quite insane and one-sided as I sought a single answer. I did not recognize that what I was seeking was something dynamic—an interplay of shades and forces and life-energies. Feng shui gives emotional and energy values to colors; cultures overlay meanings, such as white for marriages in the West and red for weddings in the East. Each day seeks a new balance, or meaning, and intuitively we seek to come into a static state, if only for an instant. Call it gratification or harmony or rest. The result is a feeling of peace and contentment.

Joy, even.

Intuitively, we know what we need, but we get used to burying this knowledge, or remembrance, and determine to think things through with our logical mind.

Of course, in terms of alchemy, sexual union is divine. The great mystery has always been how new life is created, and women have been revered above all, as they bring forth this new life. Whether mystery, magic, myth, or religion, all tell the story of wonder at birth.

The greatest embrace in the Universe is the Divine Embrace. Something has been lost from the Embrace in the past five thousand years to the Mind of God.

I'm interested in the image of the mandorla, of the space created when two circles intersect. When two perfect round shapes intersect, they create an almond-shaped space in their middle. It was the sign Christians made in the early days when greeting each other.

The shape is Pisces.

We are now beginning the Age of Aquarius. A time of water, of primal unity. A time when the cycle speaks of wholeness.

I do believe this is the signal for the return of the sacred feminine.

So much is happening. Suddenly *The Da Vinci Code* pops up—the highest-selling hardcover in five years. Millions of people are reading a story incorporating highly controversial and formerly hidden material on Mary Magdalene, the Knights Templar, and the persecution of the feminine by the Catholic Church. At dinner two nights ago, a woman of our church, who had attended a

church book-discussion on *The Da Vinci Code* said that she thought Christianity treated women just fine—look at the Virgin Mary and Mary Magdalene.

Two women. One supposedly not sexually active and the other labeled a whore.

Not a whole lot to choose from.

Chapter Two

I am now coming to understand that what is dangerous or highly controversial or subversive, like questioning the dogma of the contemporary church, may need to be written as fiction. For me, I am moving toward combining song and story or, more specifically, drawing and color, poetry, meditation, and my own deep inner truth and experience.

It took forty-five years for the Gospel of Mary to come to light. If the Dead Sea Scrolls had not been discovered, perhaps we still would not know about it. Ancient scrolls were not closely examined until the enormous cache was unearthed at Nag Hamma-di. Even though the record in the Alexandria Library in Egypt shows the existence of the scroll of the Gospel of Mary in 1896, it did not seem important to take a fresh look at the multiple strands of early Christianity. And then it took forty years for the Scrolls to be made available to the public, and that was in the face of incredible opposition and suppression by the Church.

I do believe that God acts in His way, in His time, and that now is the time for certain things to be revealed, and that the cycle is turning.

Will God restore His Shekinah, or is that for us to do?

And what is the abandonment of the feminine all about?

The three Blanchefleur roses are growing in the garden. They were fertilized today. Blanchefleur roses are a very ancient type of French rose. They are white with a red center. These are the colors of the Magdalene, the Knights Templar; these colors can be seen as symbols in many of the paintings of the Renaissance period, particularly in the works of Leonardo da Vinci.

The Supreme Symbol of the Queen of Heaven was the foliate rose. She, the living Grail.[57]

In Rosslyn Chapel, the section of the roof over the altar is carved entirely in roses. A paradise, a new Eden—one regained through sexuality and passion, through the wholeness of human connection with each other and with the divine. The Queen of Heaven, Innana, was represented by the foliate rose, as was the Magdalene. Roses and essence of rose are still considered completely feminine.

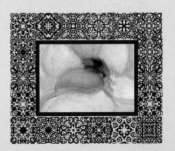

When I was at the Confluence Conference in San Francisco, I dreamt that I was part of an ancient family living in a castle in Scotland. I was trying to find the place to hang the tapestry with the dragon. The colors were red and white, the French medieval colors of the Blanchefleur. The red and white colors are the main thing. At the time, I had no idea that these harked back to Medieval times.

We are putting pink gingers and white fairy-begonias in the guest room garden. The feminine element is coming to the Knowledge corner of the house, the place I go late during the night to dream and to write. It's now three in the morning; I feel certain truths becoming self-evident.

The orange bromeliad, with its straight-up phallic shape must give up its spot by the bedside later today. I need a white orchid. The flat bedcovers have been folded away and replaced with a soft duvet.

I'm climbing into the deep feminine.

I go to the breath of God in the deep stillness.

All the clothes I have been buying lately are pink.

John O'Donohue, the poet and theologian, told me "We don't get enough of the darkness."

I believe this is true. And this is why I am so often up, writing and thinking, during the dark, quiet hours in the middle of the night.

Good writing is about telling the truth.[58] It is about our need to be heard, our need to make sense of our lives. So it's all about truth and beauty and about doing my part to restore this to my corner of the world.

I'm trying not to be afraid of my past. I'm trying to write straight into the emotional center of things.[59]

"How alive am I willing to be?"[60] I feel as if my insides are being pulled out; after a session, I feel ice-cold and completely drained.

I read that the Church of Mary was in direct opposition to the Church of Peter.

Why did this happen? I do believe that the stream of knowledge had to flow underground for some time. And now is the time for seeing the Shadow of the Living Light, to hear the Voice of Wisdom, she who has been with God from the very beginning.[61]

The time of mourning has passed, for God has declared His passion for His best beloved.[62]

You can get to the point where you see the essence of holiness in everything, a sign that God is implicit in all creation.[63] The luminosity is called into my heartbeat.

It is time to enter the lavender light.[64]

Chapter Three

I am tired of all this talk about shame. I never changed when I was told that I was born a sinner. Women have attended births since time immemorial, and I dare you to tell me that the little one coming into the world is bad, or that the woman giving birth and taking care of her newborn is bad. Women shed their blood as part of the process of bringing new life into the world, and without this gift the divine presence would cease. The desire of the man and the woman in the Garden was for knowledge, and the serpent, often known as the wise-woman in disguise, gave it to them.

Who says that this knowledge is evil?

The knowledge, it seems to me, has to do with nakedness and sexuality, and there was a common language understood between humans and animals and God. We have forgotten, or have been taught to forget, our true nature, the one that has the spark of the divine in it. The one that has to do with light and union and wholeness.

In the *Pistis Sophia*, the Pistis herself creates God, a shadow within her light. And He, then, creates the world and forgets that He is part of a greater whole.

The cache of documents at Nag Hammadi, as well as the Dead Sea Scrolls, support the Gnostic interpretation of the stories of creation, of our origins. The Gospel of Thomas, the Gospel of Mary, and the Gospel of Peter all point to the fact that Mary

Magdalene was a historical figure of the highest order, a divine priestess destined to unite with Jesus, to bring his message to a plane of mystical knowledge. There was a struggle between Peter and Mary Magdalene. The Catholic Church as we know it today held on to the personage of Peter as the founding rock of Christianity and rejected Mary Magdalene as an insignificant figure.

Some believe that Jesus was an Essene; others say that He was a mystery teacher from Egypt. And yet others talk of the uniting of his branch of David with the Mary Magdalene branch of Benjamin, thus making a true King of the Jews.[65]

Without the discovery of the Gospel of Mary in 1888, and then the Nag Hammadi and Dead Sea Scroll discoveries fifty years later, all this early struggle and history would have been buried. And, with it, the richness and diversity of beliefs of the first centuries A.D.

There is no one truth. There are many and, in imagining the possibilities, I feel my mind and my heart open up.

And that, I believe, is why Mary Magdalene has been holding her power behind Mary, the Mother of Jesus, for so long.

If I am to respect the freedom and dignity of other human beings, then this openness to multiple possibilities is essential. It is not for me to control how other people think and believe. My role is to open myself spiritually and to lay out what is true for me, hoping it may be useful for another.

The Gnostics believe that divinity is immanent within the human spirit. Their view of the world is based in myth, not in theology, and perhaps that is why stories have as much resonance for me as do works of fiction. I have had a dream—over

and over—in which I have heard a voice telling me "You have the power to write myths," and that is the voice I am listening to.

I pray to have presence and to bear witness.

Before there was the sun, moon, and stars, there was light.

I am the remembrance of the fullness.[66]

Am I living a life of beauty? Of memory?

Of art, poetry, landscape? Of the old trees?

I talk with the life around me. In the morning, I speak with the fishes when I give them their food. Yesterday, after the heavy rains, there was a small white heron fishing in the puddle on North County Road. I said, "Hello, how beautiful you are," as I was passing.

Perhaps the goddess at the heart of creation does not want to be revealed. She is secret and silent and chooses to remain so.

I ask myself, "What is the dream story, the beauty story, the vision story that I want to move in to?"

I read that there is something about the death of someone you love that shatters your life, and that you will never be the same again. This is so. Especially at this time of year, I think of Bert, of how I have now lived twice as many years as he did, and of what he missed with his three little children. I look at Rob and Laura with Sonia, and know that he had Leslie for even less time than they have had with their daughter. I remember how he loved Chris, and the laughter and games and cozy holding times. The memory hurts less on a regular basis, but when it comes back it is so sharp and just twists deep inside. Memory of loss does not go away.

John O'Donohue speaks of the darkness, and of how we do not get enough of it. The darkness does teach me where the wound is; in the night I go into that place, and do not run from it. I don't wallow, but I do know how deep and how awesome the hole of loss is.

Chapter Four

he "Sleeping Lady" in the National Archeology Museum in Valletta, Malta, is the priestess sleeping in a sacred cave, visited by prophetic dreams.[67] Guarding the Grail of the earth; dreaming her dreams of our lives.

I believe in human goodness.

I believe in a new Garden of Eden, where sexuality can be accepted without shame, where it is part of our nature, and part of nature.

Am I a Messenger of Light?

Am I in touch with the knowledge of the heart?

When I look at Thomas Cole's painting "Garden of Eden," I feel so comfortable there. In my mind, in my imagination, this is a place I can go. The sense of beauty suffuses my soul. There is a mythic world that exists for me, and it is one of "perpetual greenness," in the words of Hildegard of Bingen. Whether or not immortality is part of it does not worry me. I do not fear death; it just feels like part of the cycle of growth and decay and rebirth, all for the nourishment and perpetuation of the earth.

I felt that Jane arrived as Mike's mom left; perhaps Sonia has Winifred's spirit, or Bonnie's. These are either our family members or close friends—people in our life who are passing in and out of this world.

Where are the poets, the bards, the visionaries who gave us the Song of Songs?

Is there space, in this time of computers and cell phones, of cars and business and fragmented lives, to remember about

Light and Light-giving love? Is it just with the little ones, who come as gifts?

Can I call the luminosity into my heartbeat?

Paradise as a walled garden. How many people have responded to the photograph of me sitting in our garden; I believe it has to do with peace and beauty and a direction of energy. Mike says that the photographer, Greer Garson, captured the earthbound spirit of both me and the garden.

I'm happy with the results. For if green spaces—constructed, in this case—are for prayer and meditation, then for both of us our plan of shaping the environment to support this stage of our lives is being carried out.

The enclosed space at home is, of course, a secret place, and we invite in only those we want to share it with.

Dickinson bloomed in solitude, in her garden, and with her huge manuscript collections of pressed flowers.

And God said, Let the earth bring forth grass, the herb yielding seed, and the fruit tree yielding fruit after his kind, whose seed is in itself, upon the earth: and it was so.

And the earth brought forth grass and herb yielding seed after his kind, and the tree yielding fruit, whose seed was in itself, after his kind: and God saw that it was good.

(Genesis 1:11–12, King James Version)

In the Garden there was not only the communication between animal and human, and animal and human and God, but also the complete unity of the Creator—the original androgyny, as it were. The garden was created on the third day and was followed by the creatures that were to inhabit it.

What was in the mind of God, in our creation story, to disrupt this original unity? That, to me, seems to be the question. And if, as pagan religions believe, the sexual act restores the original androgyny, why were Eve and Adam thrown out of the Garden before anything happened between them?[68]

What, then, was the purpose of God's creation, if there was to be no reproduction, no continuation of the species? Was God Himself going to keep making more of us?

Or is this all a construction of those who wrote the texts and recorded certain versions of the Story into the Bible as we know it?

Interesting, to turn the story around.

The quest for Gnostic, feminine wisdom is in opposition to the Story. For in the former, the belief is that all of us are good, all of us have the divine spark within us, and our purpose here on earth is to come into ever greater and deeper contact with that divine spark, and to know our creator.

There is a beautiful book in the Nag Hammadi horde. It is called "On the Origin of the World," and the creation story is retold. Before God there was a light in the Chaos, and she was

called the Pistis Sophia. There was immeasurable light everywhere, but there was a shadow who existed on the outside. The
Pistis saw this shadow moving in the depth of the waters and
she called to it, but he did not see her face—he saw only himself
and thought that he alone existed.

The story goes on and becomes quite complicated, but in it Sophia sent her daughter, Eve, to instruct Adam, who had no soul.
When Adam rose up and opened his eyes, he saw her and said,
"You will be called the mother of the living, because you are the
one who gave me life."[69]

 hapter Five

The woman chooses when and on whom she bestows her blessing.[70] By sharing her energy and power with a man, she blesses and empowers him.

"My new song must float like a feather on the breath of God."[71]

A ministering priestess with a deep understanding of the thresholds of the spirit world.[72]

"When her tears were spent, Jacob held her to his chest until it seemed she was asleep, and told her that she was the moon's own daughter, luminous, radiant, and perfect."

(*The Red Tent* by Diamant)

"For as long as he lived, I walked with him by day and lay down with him at night."

(Rebecca, *The Red Tent*)

And here is where I move beyond words, into the poetry of others. I think of the gifts my husband gives me, how he held me when I grieved over Bonnie's death, and how the joy of human touch is healing and beyond.

And I think of what I can do for him, if I were to leave here before him. This morning we went and picked out a place for our ashes to rest on the east wall of the columbarium at Bethesda-by-the-Sea. There is a bench before our spot, and it's a place where the energy and peace of the natural world seem to touch one's soul. And, yes, I will stay by your side as long as you need me.

"Night lasts as long as day, and we live with the nighttime also."[73]

Am I living a life of beauty?

"…but only (as) wise-woman, priestess, Lady-of-the-Lake."[74]

"The Queen of Heaven, the true wife of the sky-god…she, too, loves the solitude of the woods and the lonely hills, and sailing overhead on clear nights in the likeness of the silver moon she looked down with pleasure on her own fair image reflected on the calm, the burnished surface of the lake, Diana's mirror."[75]

Epilogue

The temple of the sylvan goddess, indeed, has vanished, and the King of the Wood no longer stands sentinel over the Golden Bough. But Nemi's woods are still green, and as the sunset fades above them in the west, there comes to us, borne on the swell of the wind, the sound of the church bells of Ariccia, ringing the Angelus. *Ave Maria!* Sweet and solemn they chime out from the distant town, and die lingeringly away across the wide Campagnan marshes. *Le roi est mort, vive le roi! Ave Maria!*

(Frazer, *Balder*, Volume II, 308–309)

ACKNOWLEDGMENT

All photos are of artwork by Dora Frost. She visualizes what I write about; her paintings move my thoughts forward. Her images are like my words, and yet, the one is better with the other, for language needs the fuller senses to truly speak to us.

My husband, Mike, my friends, and readers, Jenny, Ros, Rebecca, and Dora all help me to believe in what I am trying to do. Thank you.

Note on the photographs:

Taken in Africa, 1997, by the author

# Bibliography

The Genesis Garden

Begg, Ean. *The Cult of the Black Virgin*. London: Penguin Books, 1985.

Bennett, Paula. *My Life a Loaded Gun: Dickinson, Plath, Rich, and Female Creativity*. Chicago: University of Illinois Press, 1990.

Bradley, Marion Zimmer. *The Mists of Avalon*. New York: The Ballantine Publishing Group, 1982.

Brock, Ann Graham. *Mary Magdalene, the First Apostle: The Struggle for Authority*. Cambridge, Massachusetts: Harvard University Press, 2003.

Brown, Dan. *The Da Vinci Code*. New York: Doubleday, 2003.

Conway, Hugh. *Called Back*. Chicago: Rand, McNally & Co., 1884.

Diamant, Anita. *The Red Tent*. New York: St. Martin's Press, 1997.

Franklin, R.W., ed. *The Manuscript Books of Emily Dickinson, Vol. I & II*. Cambridge, Massachusetts: The Belknap Press, 1981.

Frazer, James. *The Golden Bough, Vol. I–XII*. 3rd ed. New York: The MacMillan Company, 1935.

Habegger, Alfred. *My Wars Are Laid Away in Books: The Life of*

Emily Dickinson. New York: Random House, 2001.

Johnson, Robert A. *He: Understanding Masculine Psychology*. New York: Harper & Row, Publishers, 1989.

——*Owning Your Own Shadow: Understanding the Dark Side of the Psyche*. San Francisco: Harper San Francisco, 1991.

Johnson, Thomas H., ed. *Emily Dickinson: Selected Letters*. Cambridge, Massachusetts: The Belknap Press, 1971.

——*The Complete Poems of Emily Dickinson*. Boston: Little, Brown and Company, 1957.

Jung, C.G. *Modern Man in Search of a Soul*. Translated by W.S. Dell and Cary F. Baynes. New York: Harcourt Brace & Company, first published in 1933.

Khashoggi, Soheir. *Mirage*. New York: Forge Press, 1996.

King, Karen L. *What is Gnosticism?* Cambridge, Massachusetts: The Belknap Press, 2003.

——. Minneapolis: Fortress Press, 1997.

Lachman, Barbara. *The Journal of Hildegard of Bingen.* New York: Bell Tower, 1993.

Lamott, Anne. *Bird by Bird: Some Instructions on Writing and Life.* New York: Pantheon Books, 1994.

Leloup, Jean-Yves, trans. *The Gospel of Mary Magdalene.* Rochester, Vermont: Inner Traditions, 2002.

Meehan, Bernard. *The Book of Kells: An Illustrated Introduction to The Manuscript in Trinity College Dublin.* London: Thames and Hudson, 1994.

Mernissi, Fatema. *Scheherazade Goes West: Different Cultures, Different Harems.* New York: Washington Square Press, 2001.

Merton, Thomas. *The Other Side of the Mountain: The End of the Journey.* San Francisco: Harper San Francisco, 1998.

Meyer, Marvin W., trans. *The Gospel of Thomas: the Hidden Sayings of Jesus.* San Francisco: Harper San Francisco, 1992.

——*The Secret Teachings of Jesus: Four Gnostic Gospels*. New York: Vintage Books, 1984.

Miller, Cristanne. *Emily Dickinson: A Poet's Grammar*. Cambridge, Massachusetts: Harvard University Press, 1987.

Pagels, Elaine. *Beyond Belief: The Secret Gospel of Thomas*. New York: Random House, 2003.

Red Star, Nancy. *Star Ancestors: Indian Wisdomkeepers Share the Teachings of the Extraterrestrials*. Rochester, Vermont: Destiny Books, 2000.

Robinson, James M., ed. *The Nag Hammadi Library in English*. New York: Harper & Row, Publishers, 1977.

Sansom, C.J. *Dissolution: a novel of Tudor England*. New York: Viking, 2003.

Sewall, Richard B. *The Life of Emily Dickinson*, New York: Farrar, Strauss and Giroux, 1974.

Shanks, Hershel, ed. *Understanding the Dead Sea Scrolls: A*

Reader from the *"Biblical Archaeology Review."* New York: Random House, 1993.

Sinclair, Andrew. *The Sword and the Grail.* New York: Crown Publishers, 1992.

Vermes, Geza, trans. *The Complete Dead Sea Scrolls in English.* New York: The Penguin Press, 1997.

Wilkinson, Richard H. *The Complete Temples of Ancient Egypt.* New York: Thames and Hudson, 2000.

Wolkstein, Diane and Kramer, Samuel Noah. *Inanna: Queen of Heaven and Earth, Her Stories and Hymns from Sumer.* New York: Harper & Row, Publishers, 1983.

Papers:

Confluence Conference, San Francisco, notes

The Gnostic World View: A Brief Summary of Gnosticism

Translation notes, Darby Translation, Genesis 1

Translation notes, King James Version, Genesis 1, 3

Victor, Wendy F. "The Power and Passion of Emily Dickinson."

notes

PART III

WINGS OF THE CHERUBIM

t's all about the old trees.

Ethiopia was once a land of trees. Deeply forested, replete with all kinds of animals and birds, the lushness of the vegetation marked the birthplace of the human race. Called the Cradle of Civilization, flying in with a small plane, the image today is brown on brown on brown. Steep ravines, impossible plateaus, and side hills cut into small fields bordered by rock fences. Here the boys tend their goats, seeking the most meager of existences. Girls are not allowed to stray so far from the villages, for fear of rape and murder.

Instead, they become beasts of burden, picking up stray sticks from the periphery of the village, loading these huge bundles on their backs, and bringing home the fuel for cooking.

Gradually the stones take over. The earth is parched by drought. Shade is as scarce as food. Families need more and more children to perform the labor to keep the daily work done. Girls marry as early as twelve years old and have as many as eighteen children.

A harsh life in a harsh land. It is a stronghold of the Christian faith in Africa, and it is here that, according to legend, the Ark of the Covenant was brought from the Temple of Solomon.

Lalibela is the holy place. Eleven churches are cut down into the stone; the Church of Mary is at the center of the complex. Built in the eleventh century, this is a huge center of pilgrimage. Women, men, and children walk for months up and down the ra-

vines and across the stony plateaus to come here to worship for the Feast of the Ascension. A week, perhaps, in Lalibela, and then the long walk home.

Holy men live here in caves built in the walls of these subterranean churches. Their entire life can take place within a space two feet high and three feet wide. When they die, the holy bones are left in place.

The stories of creation are different here from the ones I am used to from the Book of Genesis. Instead of God creating by Himself and with His Word, here the animals and birds

of the woods cluster about a Fountain of Life. Creation is an act of joy and of nature, and the holiness of the mystery takes place in an open-air pavilion.

The only patches of green in this land-scape are in the monasteries. The old trees here could never be cut down; this is the only glimpse of the land as it once was.

Vibrant, alive in the virtual desert, it is a place where women come to worship, to re-new themselves in this place of peace. They literally touch the wood of the doors with their lips as they enter the holy grounds.

The reverence for wood, for the old trees, for their past, is palpable. The energy flows into them and reunites them to a lost world.

A world of mystery, strength, and of for-gotten greenness.

I think of these things as we travel in Af-rica with the American Museum of Natural

History. I think of how the women here are so strong, how they are learning to speak out for themselves, unite, and slowly find a voice. The Internet is connecting them. I can go to web sites and see the price of grain in different villages in Mali, giving me knowledge of where is the best place to trade for profit or for fresh seeds.

In Somalia, after the Women's Conference "On Stopping Ten Years of Civil Violence," held in the spring of 2001, a pamphlet was published with not only all the papers presented, but with the e-mail addresses of the presenters listed at the back.

This is how the tapestry is woven.

Wherever I go, I talk with the local women. I believe it makes a difference letting my hair be gray. How can

I speak to them if I am not comfortable with who I am?

In Tunisia, in the Museum at Carthage, I am struck by the images of strong women. Poseidon rises out of the sea with a female consort by his side. Centaurs are female, as are the Goddesses in the Garden.

The female body is strong and beautiful. She brings fertility to the land. She feeds her people and produces life.

And, once again, she is at the heart of creation.

So much history is changed, rewritten. The stories of our strength, our power—our blessing that is at the heart of life—are being forgotten. With the rise of patriarchy and male violence (indeed, the very definition of manhood being based on guns and conquest and aggression), the stories are only being whispered in the dark.

One of the myths of Africa that came un-glued for me happened in the land of Zambia. I had started to create universals out of the little I had seen; I thought all Africa was bar-ren, deforested; that the greenness and well-ness was a thing of the past. Then we came into this village, and there was this incredible lushness—crops growing everywhere in rich alluvial soil.

Children had fat cheeks; they were laughing and smiling. None were left alone—little ones carried littler ones around with them.

The sense of community is some-thing we have so lost here.

So I am rethinking what we have in the West, in our supposedly advanced and civilized way of life, and of what we can learn from Africa.

Still, I have just been in the villages.

The women are shy when talking to me. I look and listen—to the sounds of their voices as they talk together, to the local music, to the birds, to the sound of heavy rain, and to crickets in the night.

In three weeks, I heard only one child cry.

Amazing what this sense of community can do.

But, then, there is the ugliness of war and of displaced persons and of the incred-

ible contrasts of wealth and of ways of life. Leaving Victoria Falls, we boarded the Blue Train, heading for South Africa and Capetown. Camera in hand, I strolled into the dining car. Coming from the thatched huts and dirt floors of the village in Zambia, the linen and silver on the table took my breath away. Incredibly rich food was laid out before us.

During the long night, the cars swayed on the tracks, lulling us into the rhythm of the journey south. And, in the first light of

dawn, what a sight there was. Slums, stretching as far as the eye could see, with rolls of barbed wire stuck on top of the walls.

How on earth do I talk to these people? And what to say or ask or do?

Of course, I could not. Penetration into their space would be a violation and would not be forgiven.

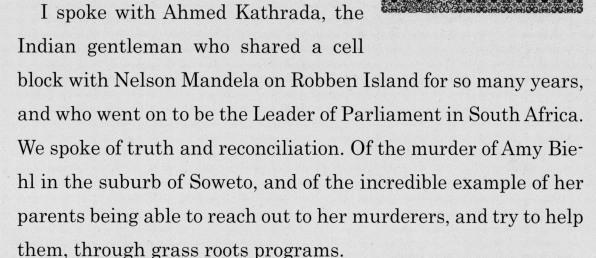

I spoke with Ahmed Kathrada, the Indian gentleman who shared a cell block with Nelson Mandela on Robben Island for so many years, and who went on to be the Leader of Parliament in South Africa. We spoke of truth and reconciliation. Of the murder of Amy Biehl in the suburb of Soweto, and of the incredible example of her parents being able to reach out to her murderers, and try to help them, through grass roots programs.

I believe in essential goodness. In the truth and beauty and light deep inside each of us, and of our responsi-

bility to help bring this out. It seems an overwhelming task at times, but light attracts light, and the people working in this way attract each other and reinforce each other.

When I was organizing a symposium on Educating Women for Peace in Connecticut, I asked Cokie Roberts, TV anchorwoman, to be one of the panelists. I wanted a strong voice from the media who would speak up about gender images and gender choices,

and how what we see and hear about women affects how we feel about ourselves.

To my incredible surprise, Cokie Roberts answered that she saw no need for change. She felt women had made so many advances over the past years and there were no issues left to address.

So I found a friend of my husband's, who was head of another national news station, and he was a husband and father of several daughters. He felt that female images and understanding of our self-worth had a long way to go, and he served as a strong advocate for change on our panel.

I keep coming back to the old trees. The light and the mystery.

There is a beautiful botanical garden in Capetown. Nestled behind Table Mountain, it is filled with fragrance, wisps of fog, and hanging clouds. It is a place of beauty at the tip of Africa.

Women's work. It is the heart of Africa.

In the parched landscape of Mali, in the Dogon country, women's labor is the method of irrigation. Pot by pot, they carry water by hand to nourish the crops. The desert stands at bay, at the edge of the flatland.

Miraculously, the trees survive.

Women are the ones who market the vegetables and the fruits. They are the life of the people.

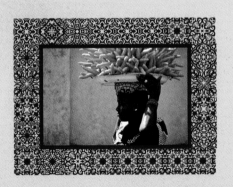

Epilogue

How far have I come from the Amazon, from the journey into the darkness, from the choice to stand in silence? And what happened to the move into poetry and art, and into the lavender light of holiness?

I went to Africa to look for the strength of women. My dream of the two children of Solomon and the Queen of Sheba made me believe there was something holy in the place of our earliest beginnings. What started as an exploration to bring women's history into my school turned out, for me, to be a travel back to my own roots. I was forced to leave my preconceived Western notions behind if I was to see and hear and learn from others.

From ancient times up to the present, I find women at the heart of the life of their people. It does not surprise me that astonishing women in Africa are coming into political power, are at the forefront of environmental movements, and are banding together to stop civil war, lawlessness, and unbelievable violence on the part of the men. These women believe in their place in the story of creation. They have a strength that I can only admire and emulate and seek to bring to my people.

It is We who are the Cherubim;
It is We who guard the gates of Paradise,
And hover over the Ark,
Protecting, Blessing,
Bringing forth life in darkness,
And taking it away.

For long, oh so long,
We have been silent
Standing behind the Mystery,
Choosing to let our sons
Wage wars, make polis,
Write their stories, and create their gods.

But now the breath of life flickers
And almost dies. It no longer moves
Over the living waters.

O my Soul, take courage,
Step forth from behind Thy Ark.
Bless us and restore us and make us whole again.

Bring us back, O Divine One
Into Thy Luminous Heartbeat.

Postscript

In December 2008 the author and her husband are planning to return to Africa.

Note on the photographs:

Taken in Africa, 1997, by the author.

Bibliography

WINGS OF THE CHERUBIM

Amundsen, Christian. *Insights from the Secret Teachings of Jesus: The Gospel of Thomas.* Fairfield, Iowa: Sunstar Publishing, 1998.

Armstrong, Karen. *Buddha.* New York: Viking Books, 2001.

Baigent, Michael. *The Jesus Papers: Exposing the Greatest*

Cover-Up in History. San Francisco: Harper San Francisco, 2006.

Barber, Richard. *The Holy Grail: Imagination and Belief.* Cambridge, Massachusetts: Harvard University Press, 2004.

Berry, Steve. *The Templar Legacy: A Novel.* New York: Ballantine Books, 2006.

Bleiberg, Edward. *Tree of Paradise: Jewish Mosaics from the Roman Empire.* New York: Brooklyn Museum, 2006.

Brown, Michele P., ed. *In the Beginning: Bibles before the Year 1000.* Washington D.C.: Smithsonian Institution Press, 2006.

Campbell, Joseph. *Myths to Live By.* New York: The Viking Press, 1972.

Chance, Jane, ed. *Tolkien and the Invention of Myth: A Reader.* Lexington, Kentucky: The University Press of Kentucky, 2004.

Coogan, Michael D., ed. *The New Oxford Annotated Bible, Third Edition, with the Apocryphal/Deuteroncanonical Books.* Oxford, England: Oxford University Press, 2001.

Cooper, Guy and Taylor, Gordon. *Mirrors of Paradise: The Gardens of Fernando Caruncho.* New York: The Monacelli Press, 2000.

Cowart, Jack. *Matisse in Morocco: The Paintings and Drawings, 1912–1913.* Washington, D.C.: National Gallery of Art, 1990.

De Boron, Robert. *Merlin and the Grail: Joseph of Arimathea, Merlin, Perceval.* Translated by Nigel Bryant. Cambridge: D.S. Brewer, 2001. (Written in the 13th century.)

Degas, Edgar. *A Degas Sketchbook: The Halevy Sketchbook, 1877–1883.* New York: Dover Publications, 1988.

Eliot, T.S. *The Wasteland and Other Writings.* New York: The Modern Library, 2001. First published in 1922.

Evan, Helen C., ed. *Byzantium: Faith and Power (1261–1557)*. New York: Metropolitan Museum of Art, 2004.

Farr, Judith. *The Gardens of Emily Dickinson*. Cambridge, Massachusetts: Harvard University Press, 2004.

Friedman, Thomas L. *The World is Flat: A Brief History of the Twenty-First Century*. New York: Farrar, Straus and Giroux, 2005.

Hantelmann, Christa von, ed. *Gardens of Delight: The Great Islamic Gardens*. DoMont Buchverlag, Köln, 2001.

Hobbs, Anne Stevenson. *Beatrix Potter's Art: Paintings and Drawings*. London: The Penguin Group, 1989.

Hussein, Shamis I., Project Coordinator. *Conflict Resolution, Confidence-Building and Peace Enhancement among Somali Women*. Workshop organized in Somaliland. United Nations Press, 2001.

Johnson, Robert A. *Balancing Heaven and Earth: a memoir of visions, dreams, and realizations*. San Francisco: Harper San Francisco, 1998.

——*We: Understanding the Psychology of Romantic Love.* San Francisco: Harper San Francisco, 1983.

Jung, Emma and von Franz, M.-L. *The Grail Legend.* New York: G.P. Putnam's Sons, 1970. (English translation first published by the Jung Foundation.)

Lewis, C.S. *The Lion, the Witch, and the Wardrobe.* The Chronicles of Narnia. New York: Harper Collins Publisher, 1950.

Nelson, Robert S. *Hagia Sophia, 1850–1950, Holy Wisdom Modern Monument.* Chicago: The University of Chicago Press, 2004.

Nickel, Lucas, ed. *Return of the Buddha: The Quingzhou Discoveries.* London: Royal Academy of Arts, 2002.

Rossi, Corinna. *The Treasures of the Monastery of Saint Catherine.* Verecelli, Italy: White Star Publishing, 2006.

Sierra, Javier. *The Secret Supper.* New York: Atria Books, 2004.

Smoley, Richard. *Forbidden Faith: The Gnostic Legacy from the*

Gospels to "The Da Vinci Code." New York: Harper San Francisco, 2006.

The Holy Bible: Illuminated Family Edition, King James Version. Atlanta, Georgia: Lionheart Books, 2000.

Tuchman, Barbara W. *A Distant Mirror: The Calamitous 14th Century.* New York: Alfred A. Knopf, 1978.

Venolia, Carol. *Healing Environments: Your Guide to Indoor Well-Being.* Berkeley, California: Celestial Arts, 1988.

Wilson, Ian. *Before the Flood: The Biblical Flood as a Real Event and How it changed the Course of Civilization.* New York: St. Martin's Press, 2002.

Papers:

Victor, Wendy F., "Cultural arrogance and the work of benevolence: Women writers' attempts to reform Indian policy in the New Republic, 1824–1884." Bronxville, New York: Sarah Lawrence College, 1995.

——"Educating Women for Peace: Looking Forward from Beijing." Greenwich, Connecticut: Convent of the Sacred Heart, 1996.

OTES

Epigraph

John G. Neihardt, *Black Elk Speaks*, (New York: William Morrow, 1932) 3–4, quoted in Johnson, *We: Understanding the Psychology of Romantic Love*, 175.

Five Thousand Years of Silence

(Endnotes)

[1] Katz, *Messengers of the Wind*, 56.

[2] Lerner, *The Creation of Patriarchy*, 160.

[3] Ibid., 126.

[4] Wilson, *From Atlantis to the Sphinx*, 219

[5] Abram, *The Spell of the Sensuous*, 99; Wilson, *From Atlantis to the Sphinx*, 249.

[6] Lerner, *The Creation of Patriarchy*, 149.

[7] Wilson, *From Atlantis to the Sphinx*, 250.

[8] Abram, *The Spell of the Sensuous*, 97.

[9] Estes, *Women Who Run with the Wolves*, 19.

[10] Buss, *Forged Under the Sun*, 279.

[11] Wilson, *From Atlantis to the Sphinx*, 327.

[12] Scholem, *On the Kabbalah,* 108.

[13] Lerner, *The Creation of Feminist Consciousness,* 248.

[14] Lerner, *The Creation of Patriarchy,* 186.

[15] Ibid., 186

[16] Genesis 1:26–27; Genesis 2:18–24.

[17] Pope, *Song of Songs,* 192.

[18] Ibid., 145.

[19] Ibid., 113–114, 145.

[20] Ibid., 167, 227.

[21] Ibid., 157.

[22] Young, *An Anthology of Sacred Texts,* 55. The Gospel of Mary was found in the library in Alexandria, Egypt, about one hundred years ago, but was not given importance in the history of early Christianity until after the discovery and reading of the Dead Sea Scrolls.

23 Gilligan, *In a Different Voice,* xiii.

24 Young, *An Anthology of Sacred Texts,* 253; Abram, *The Spell of the Sensuous,* 166, 172.

25 Scholem, *On the Kabbalah,* 108; Abram, *The Spell of the Sensuous,* 196.

26 Lawlor, *Sacred Geometry,* 16.

27 Young, *An Anthology of Sacred Texts,* 55; Lachman, *The Journal of Hildegard of Bingen,* cited in Part II. Hildegard of Bingen was a twelfth-century abbess, mystic, and writer; Lerner, *The Creation of Feminist Consciousness,* 63.

28 Scholem, *On the Kabbalah,* ix.

29 Wall, *Wisdom's Daughters,* 302.

30 Bonheim, *Goddess: A Celebration,* 90.

31 Lerner, *The Creation of Feminist Consciousness,* 181.

32 Gilligan, *In a Different Voice,* xix-xx.

33 Lerner, *Why History Matters*, 127.

34 Young, *An Anthology of Sacred Texts*, 255 (emphasis mine); Davidson, *From Alice to Ocean*, 124, 127.

35 Bonheim, *Goddess: A Celebration*, 8.

36 Gilligan, *In a Different Voice*, xi.

37 Young, *An Anthology of Sacred Texts*, xi.

38 Wall, *Wisdom's Daughters*, xi.

39 Brown, *The Sacred Pipe*, 83.

40 Chang, *The Rape of Nanking*, 7.

41 Young, *An Anthology of Sacred Texts*, xi.

42 Ibid., xxi.

43 McNamara, *Sisters in Arms*, 37.

44 Young, *An Anthology of Sacred Texts*, xviii.

45 Helman, *African Zion*, 11.

46 Ibid.

[47] Young, *An Anthology of Sacred Texts*, xxvi.

[48] Ibid., 41.

[49] Ibid., 49.

[50] Scholem, *On the Kabbalah*, 96, 105; Young, *An Anthology of Sacred Texts*, 49.

[51] Young, *An Anthology of Sacred Texts*, 55, 70.

[52] Ibid., 274.

[53] Estes, *Women Who Run with the Wolves*, 12; Buss, *Forged Under the Sun*, 62.

The Genesis Garden

[54] Jung believes that women have a masculine side, the animus, and men have their feminine side, the anima. Until peace is made with the inner opposite, there is continual unrest and discontent.

[55] Johnson, *We,* 28–29. In the tale of "Parsifal," who was a knight of Arthur's Round Table, Parsifal must perform his heroic deeds for Blanche Fleur. She is his lady fair and the carrier of inspiration; Frazer, *The Golden Bough,* I, 25. Aphrodite's own tree, in the sacred woods of Nemi, has red and white blossoms.

[56] Bradley, *The Mists of Avalon,* x. I like her use of the term, and her spelling.

[57] Sinclair, *The Sword and the Grail,* 44. The cult of Mary Magdalene reached Scotland. The principal room at Rosslyn Chapel, Edinburgh, has a stone ceiling carved entirely of roses.

[58] Lamott, *Bird by Bird,* 3. She has given me the courage to write this book.

[59] Merton, *The Other Side of the Mountain,* 51. In his spiritual journey, Thomas Merton constantly challenged himself to let go of external things and to experience life at its core essence.

[60] Lamott, *Bird by Bird,* 236.

[61] Lachman, *The Journal of Hildegard Bingen*, 31. In reference to Lucifer and his battle with Yahweh, and to Lucifer's seeing yet another light, one whom he called "the living light."

[62] Ibid., 137. Referring to Wisdom, she who has been with God since the very beginning.

[63] Lamott, *Bird by Bird*, 100.

[64] Redstar, *Star Ancestors*, 118, 161. Nancy Redstar is a friend of mine. She is an Indian Wisdomkeeper; I find great inspiration and truth in her work. As she explains in her writings, purple is the highest of the chakras, the color of those most spiritually advanced. Light colors, in this case lavender, are even more spiritual than the deeper colors.

[65] Leloup, *The Gospel of Mary Magdalene*, xv; Brock, *Mary Magdalene, The First Apostle*, 60, 96; Pagels, *Beyond Belief*, 63; Begg, *The Cult of the Black Virgin*, 41. These are all great references for the points I make in this section.

[66] First line, Merton, *The Other Side of the Mountain*, 93. His challenge to himself is to have presence and to bear witness; Second line, Pagels, *Beyond Belief*, 52. From the Gnostic "Gospel of John." Here John is referring to the opening verses of Genesis; Third line, Meyer, *The Secret Teachings of Jesus*, 85. From the Gnostic "Secret Book of John," he talks about the Creation Story when the rulers stood before the Tree of Knowledge of Good and Evil.

[67] Simeti, Mary Taylor, "Before Cheops, Before Stonehenge," *New York Times*, May 12, 2002.

[68] Begg, *The Cult of the Black Virgin*, 12. The reference here is to the "greatest sacrament was the sexual act."

[69] Robinson, *The Nag Hammadi Library in English*, 111. From the Apocrypha of John; this is in reference to the story of creation, when Sophia desires to bring forth a being.

[70] King, *Women and Goddess Traditions*, 117. In Tantric Buddhism, the man is the supplicant in relation to his female partner. The male offering of sexual pleasure to the female enables her to cultivate her spiritual life and transform human pleasure into divine ecstasy (111–112).

[71] Lachman, *The Journal of Hildegard Bingen*, 47. Referring to Hildegard of Bingen, who comments on the physical act of procreation and that of Creation itself (410).

[72] Leloup, *The Gospel of Mary Magdalene*, xxi. Referring to Mary Magdalene, to her privileged use of oils to anoint Jesus, and to her being able to understand His words and meaning better than the other disciples.

[73] Jung, *Modern Man in Search of a Soul*, 219. The reference is to the value of balance, and the importance of opposites. "In daylight everything is clear..."

[74] Bradley, *The Mists of Avalon,* x. Here she is referring to the death of Arthur, and how, dying, he puts his head in her lap and sees her no longer as sister or lover or foe, but rather in her true nature.

[75] Frazer, *Balder,* Volume II, 303.